Christmas Time

for VIOLIN with Piano Accompaniment

by HARVEY S. WHISTLER

Rubank®

HAL•LEONARD® CORPORATION
7777 W BLUEMOUND RD PO BOX 13819 MILWAUKEE, WI 53213

L-267

Jingle Bells

J. PIERPONT

1131

Jolly Old Saint Nicholas

Traditional

1131

Good King Wenceslas

Old English Carol

1131

Deck the Hall

Old Welsh Air

With happiness

1131

O Little Town of Bethlehem

L. H. REDNER

1131

Silent Night

F. GRUBER

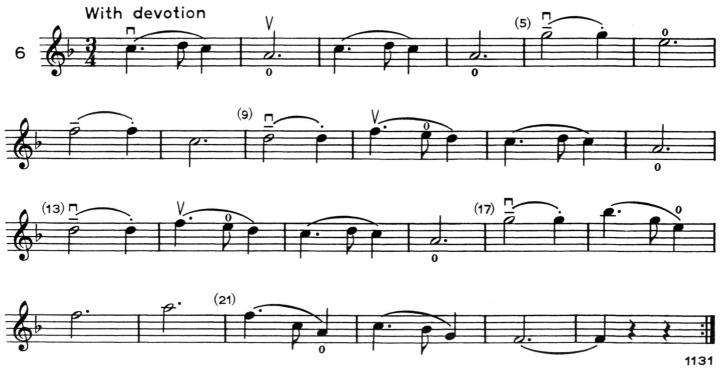

1131

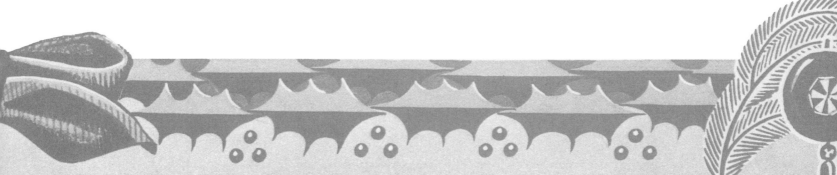

It Came Upon the Midnight Clear

R. S. WILLIS

With dignity

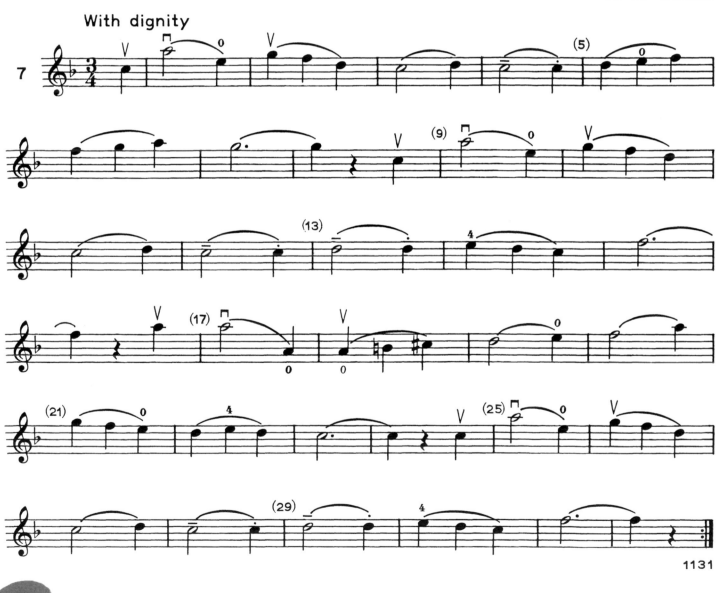

1131

PIANO ACCOMPANIMENT

Christmas Time

for VIOLIN with Piano Accompaniment
by HARVEY S. WHISTLER

RUBANK®

HAL•LEONARD®
CORPORATION
7777 W BLUEMOUND RD PO BOX 13819 MILWAUKEE, WI 53213

L-267

Jingle Bells

J. P.

J. PIERPONT

Merrily

Jin - gle bells! jin - gle bells! Jin - gle all the way!

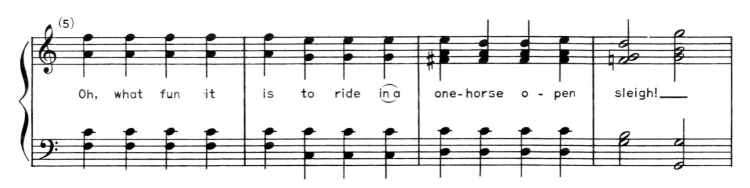

Oh, what fun it is to ride in a one-horse o - pen sleigh!___

Jin - gle bells! jin - gle bells! Jin - gle all the way!

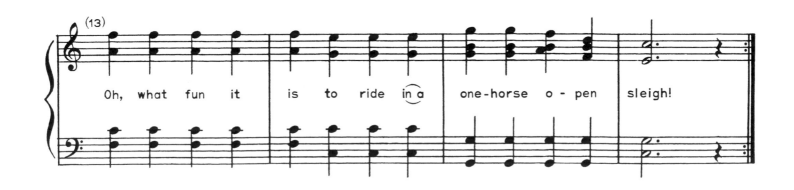

Oh, what fun it is to ride in a one-horse o - pen sleigh!

Jolly Old Saint Nicholas

Anonymous Traditional

Joyfully

1. Jol - ly old Saint | Ni - cho - las, | Lean your ear this | way!
2. When the clock is | strik - ing twelve, | When I'm fast a - | sleep,
3. John - ny wants a | pair of skates; | Su - sy wants a | sled;

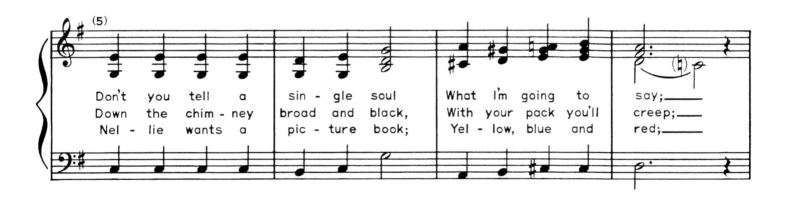

Don't you tell a | sin - gle soul | What I'm going to | say;____
Down the chim - ney | broad and black, | With your pack you'll | creep;____
Nel - lie wants a | pic - ture book; | Yel - low, blue and | red;____

Christ - mas Eve is | com - ing soon; | Now, you dear old | man,
All the stock - ings | you will find | Hang - ing in a | row;
Now I think I'll | leave to you | What to give the | rest;

Whis - per what you'll | bring to me; | Tell me if you | can.
Mine will be the | short - est one, | You'll be sure to | know.
Choose for me, dear | San - ta Claus, | You will know the | best.

Good King Wenceslas

JOHN M. NEALE

Old English Carol

4. "Sire, the night is darker now,
   And the wind blows stronger;
   Fails my heart, I know not how,
   I can go no longer."
   "Mark my footsteps, my good page,
   Tread thou on them boldly:
   Thou shalt find the winter's rage
   Freeze thy blood less coldly."

5. In his master's steps he trod,
   Where the snow lay dinted;
   Heat was in the very sod
   Which the saint had printed.
   Therefore, Christian men, be sure,
   Wealth or rank possessing,
   Ye who now will bless the poor,
   Shall yourselves find blessing.

Deck the Hall

Traditional

Old Welsh Air

With happiness

1. Deck the hall with boughs of hol - ly, Fa la la la la, la la la la.
2. See the blaz - ing Yule be - fore us, Fa la la la la, la la la la.
3. Fast a - way the old year pass - es, Fa la la la la, la la la la.

'Tis the sea - son to be jol - ly, Fa la la la la, la la la la.
Strike the harp and join the cho - rus, Fa la la la la, la la la la.
Hail the new, ye lads and lass - es, Fa la la la la, la la la la.

Don we now our gay ap - par - rel, Fa la la la la la la,
Fol - low me in mer - ry meas - ure, Fa la la la la la la,
Sing we joy - ous all to - geth - er, Fa la la la la la la,

Troll the an - cient Yule - tide car - ol, Fa la la la la, la la la la.
While I tell of Yule - tide treas - ure, Fa la la la la, la la la la.
Heed - less of the wind and weath - er, Fa la la la la, la la la la.

O Little Town of Bethlehem

P. BROOKS

L. H. REDNER

Reverently

5

1. O lit - tle town of Beth-le-hem, How still we see thee lie! A -
2. For Christ is born of Ma - ry, And gath-er'd all a - bove, While

(5)

bove thy deep and dream-less sleep The si - lent stars go by; Yet
mor - tals sleep, the an - gels keep Their watch of won-d'ring love. O

(9)

in thy dark street shin - eth The ev - er - last-ing Light; The
morn - ing stars to - geth - er Pro - claim the ho - ly birth And

(13)

hopes and fears of all the years Are met in thee to - night.
prais - es sing to God, the King, And peace to men on earth.

3. How silently, how silently,
The wondrous gift is given!
So God imparts to human hearts
The blessings of His heaven.
No ear may hear His coming,
But in this world of sin,
Where meek souls will receive Him still,
The dear Christ enters in.

4. O holy Child of Bethlehem,
Descend to us, we pray;
Cast out our sin, and enter in,
Be born in us today.
We hear the Christmas angels
The great glad tidings tell;
O, come to us, abide with us,
Our Lord Emmanuel!

1132 - 15

Silent Night

J. MOHR

F. GRUBER

It Came Upon the Midnight Clear

E. H. SEARS

R. S. WILLIS

1132 -15

We Three Kings of Orient Are

J. H. H.

J. H. HOPKINS

With zeal

1. We three Kings of O - ri - ent are;___ Bear - ing gifts we trav-erse a-
2. Born a King on Beth - le-hem's plain,___ Gold I bring to crown Him a-
3. Frank - in - cense to of - fer have I;___ In - cense owns a De - i - ty

far___ Field and foun - tain, moor and moun - tain, Fol-low-ing yon - der Star.
gain;___ King for - ev - er, ceas - ing nev - er, O-ver us all to reign.
nigh,___ Pray'r and prais - ing, all men rais - ing, Wor-ship Him God most high.

Oh,___ Star of won - der, Star of might, Star with roy - al beau - ty bright,___

West - ward lead - ing, still pro - ceed - ing, Guide us to the per - fect light.

4. Myrrh is mine; its bitter perfume
   Breathes a life of gathering gloom;
   Sorrowing, sighing, bleeding, dying,
   Sealed in the stone-cold tomb.
       Oh, Star, etc.

5. Glorious now behold Him arise,
   King and God and Sacrifice.
   Alleluia, Alleluia,
   Earth of the heavens replies.
       Oh, Star, etc.

Hark! The Herald Angels Sing

C. WESLEY

F. MENDELSSOHN

Exaltedly

9

1. Hark! the her - ald an - gels sing, _____ "Glo - ry to the new born King;
2. Christ, by high - est heav'n a - dored, _____ Christ, the ev - er - last - ing Lord,
3. Hail, the heav'n - ly Prince of Peace! _____ Hail, the Son of Right-eous-ness!

Peace on earth and mer - cy mild _____ God and sin - ner's rec - on - ciled!"
Late in time be - hold Him come, _____ Off - spring of the fa - vored one.
Light and life to all He brings, _____ Ris'n with heal - ing in His wings.

Joy - ful, all ye na - tions rise, _____ Join the tri - umph of the skies; _____
Veiled in flesh the God - head see, _____ Hail th'in - car - nate De - i - ty! _____
Mild He leaves His throne on high, _____ Born that man no more may die; _____

With th'an - gel - ic host pro - claim, "Christ is _____ born in Beth - le - hem!"
Pleased as Man with man to dwell; Je - sus, _____ our Im - man - u - el!
Born to raise the sons of earth; Born to _____ give them sec - ond birth.

Hark! the her - ald an - gels sing, "Glo - ry _____ to the new - born King!"

1132-15

O Come, All Ye Faithful

Latin Hymn, 17th Century

J. READING

God Rest You Merry, Gentlemen

Traditional

Old English Carol

3. From God, our heavenly Father,
   A blessed angel came,
   And unto certain shepherds
   Brought tidings of the same:
   How that in Bethlehem was born
   The Son of God by name.

   O tidings, etc.

4. The shepherds at those tidings,
   Rejoiced much in mind,
   And left their flocks a-feeding,
   In tempest, storm and wind,
   And went to Bethlehem straightway,
   The Son of God to find.

   O tidings, etc.

1132-15

The First Noel

Traditional

Old French Carol

4. This star drew nigh to the northwest,
   O'er Bethlehem it took its rest.
   And there it did both stop and stay,
   Right over the place where Jesus lay,
   Noel, Noel, etc.

5. Then entered in those Wisemen three.
   Full reverently upon their knee,
   And offered there, in His presence,
   Their gold and myrrh and frankincense.
   Noel, Noel, etc.

O Holy Night

A. A.

ADOLPHE ADAM

Slow and majestic

1. O ho - ly night! A star was bright-ly shin - ing, It was the
2. Led by the light of faith se - rene-ly beam - ing, With glow - ing
3. Love one an - oth - er, He did tru - ly teach us, His law is

night of the dear Sav - ior's birth; Long lay the world in sin and er - ror
hearts by His cra - dle we stand; And led by light of star so sweet-ly
love, and His gos - pel is peace; Chains shall He break for the slave is our

pin - ing, Till Christ was sent to the sin wear - y earth. A
gleam - ing, Here come the wise men from O - ri - ent land. The
broth - er, And in His name all op-pres - sion shall cease. Sweet

song of joy from all the world there ech - oes, For now there breaks a
King of kings lay thus in low - ly man - ger, In all our tri - als
hymns of joy in grate-ful cho-rus sing we, Let all with in us

14

1132 - 15

Joy to the World

I. WATTS

G. F. HANDEL

With grandeur

14

1. Joy to the world! the Lord has come: Let earth re-
2. Joy to the world! the Sav - ior reigns: Let men their

ceive her King; Let ev - 'ry____ heart____ pre - pare____ Him____
songs em - ploy; While fields__ and__ floods____ rocks, hills____ and____

room,____ And heav'n and na - ture sing, And heav'n and na - ture
plains____ Re - peat the sound - ing joy, Re - peat the sound - ing

sing, And heav'n,__ and heav'n____ and na - ture sing.
joy, Re - peat,__ re - peat____ the sound - ing joy.

3. No more let sin and sorrow grow,
Nor thorns infest the ground;
He comes to make His blessings flow
Far as the curse is found,
Far as the curse is found,
Far as, far as the curse is found.

4. He rules the world with truth and grace,
And makes the nations prove
The glories of His righteousness
And wonders of His love,
And wonders of His love,
And wonders, wonders of His love.

We Three Kings of Orient Are

J. H. HOPKINS

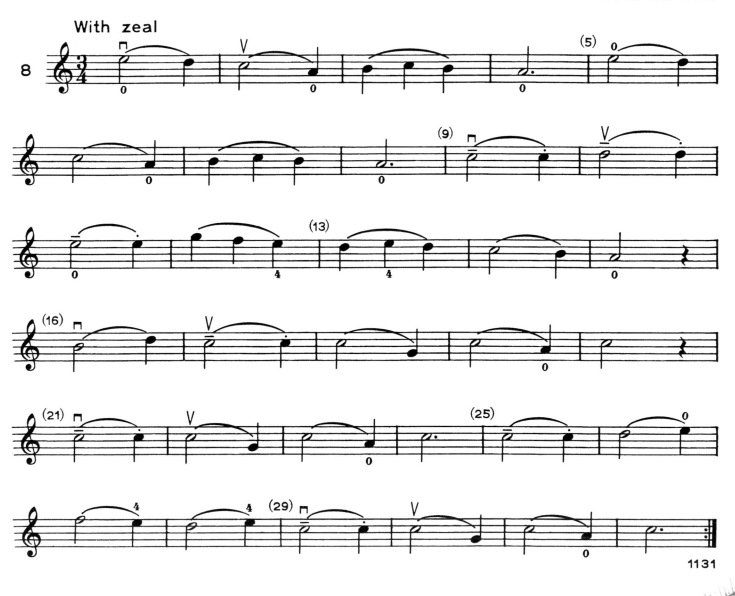

Hark! The Herald Angels Sing

F. MENDELSSOHN

9

O Come, All Ye Faithful

J. READING

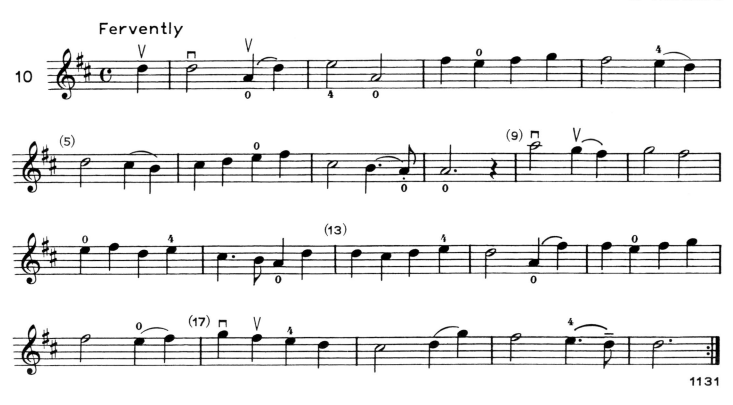

1131

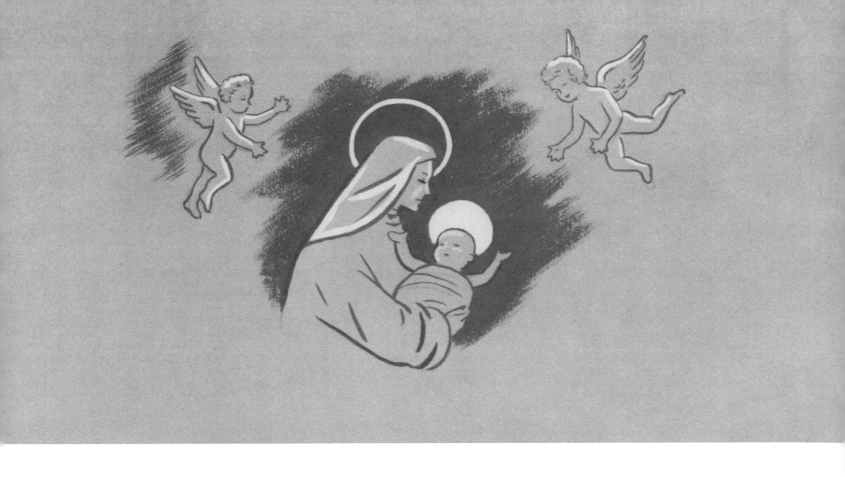

God Rest You Merry, Gentlemen

Old English Carol

The First Noel

Old French Carol

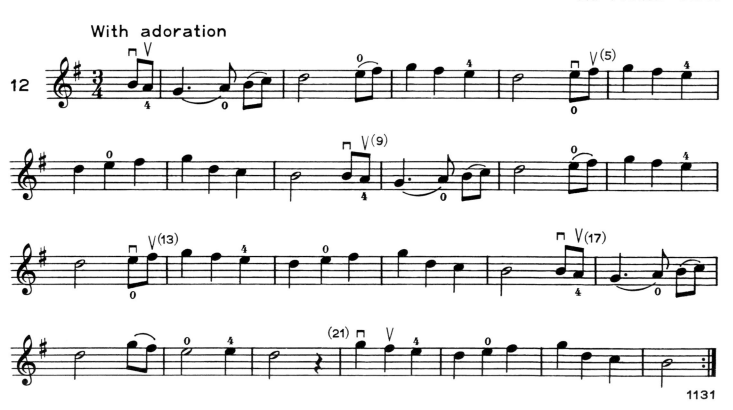

O Holy Night

ADOLPHE ADAM

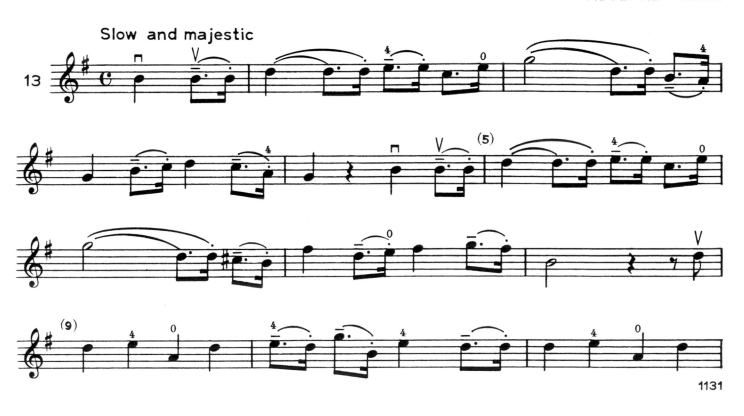

Slow and majestic

13

1131

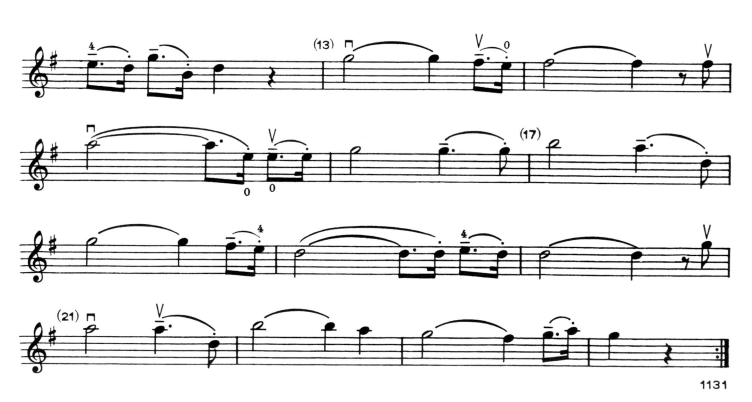

Joy to the World

G. F. HANDEL

1131